Also by E. Reid Gilbert

100 Limericks for the Final 100 Days of Trump

Whimsical Limericks from the age of Trump

100 Limericks for 100 Days of Trump

Stories Tell What Can't be Told: My Story

Shall We Gather at the River

What Matters

Valley Studio: More than a Place

The Twelve Houses of My Childhood

Trickster Jack

E. Reid Gilbert Ten Plays

100 Limericks

for the

First

100 Days

of

Biden

As Observed by
E. Reid Gilbert

A3D Impressions
Tucson | Minneapolis

100 Limericks for the First 100 Days of Biden

Copyright © 2021 E. Reid Gilbert. All rights reserved. No part of this book may be reproduced or retransmitted in any form or by any means without the written permission of the publisher.

Published by

A3D Impressions

P.O. Box 57415, Tucson, AZ 85735
www.a3dimpressions.com
a3dimpressions@gmail.com

Publisher's Cataloging-in-Publication data available

Paperback: 978-1-7371922-1-3
eBook: 978-1-7371922-2-0

David Fitzsimmons, cover and bio illustration
Donn Poll, cover and book design

Dedicated to Barbara Banks who has encouraged and supported my efforts all the way from the writing to the final production of the book. It would not have been possible without her input Barbara, my thanks.

The Limericks

In descending order.

Day B-O   1/19/21

Trump didn't show up for Biden's inauguration,
He had hoped to get himself an exoneration.
  "All charity starts at home",
  And hiding his bald dome,
He simply retreated into a temporary hibernation.

Day B-1   1/20/21

Today the presidency of Joe Biden has begun
Counting the first 100, this being day one.
   I thought it only fair
   To give Trump some air,
Biden will jump start with the starter's gun.

Day B-2   1/21/21

With Biden we must get back to some kind of norm,
Though Trump said, "I'll be back in some kind of form."
   We've had enough
   Of that kind of stuff.
We hope we're finished with the worst political storm.

Day B-3   1/22/21

President Biden is preparing for executive actions:
Hopefully resulting in various political satisfactions.
   Some national addictions
   Like party line frictions.
Some actions will be additions and others subtractions.

Day B-4   1/23/21

President Biden is preparing for executive orders
Like what is to be done with Mexican borders;
But not at all
A border wall
Though immigration is still an international disorder.

Day B-5   1/24/21

Dr. Fauci said of his reporting that made some sense,
"Everything will be based on science and evidence."
   But there'll be times
   When Gorman's rhymes
Will be deeper than the Washington political fence.

Day B-6   1/25/21

Some of the actions the former president put through
Will be changed with Biden's "Modernizing Regulations Review".
Some will love it
Others will "Shove it".
The review will have been seen by relatively few.

Day B-7   1/26/21

The "white supremacists" legacy Biden chooses to face,
The tone and implications he'd like to erase
　From legal jargon,
　And in the bargain
Consider everyone as equals in the whole human race.

Day B-8   1/27/21

Biden and his administration will promote "unity".
The GOP disdains the word with utter impunity.
It becomes plain
That Biden should explain
That political unity is basically shared community.

Day B-9   1/28/21

DHS warns that extremists continue to mobilize,
What they hope to achieve, we can only surmise.
   But who knows?
   We might suppose
That another Trump era would be their Grand Prize.

Day B-10   1/29/21

Some Republican lawmakers are making open threats
Of bodily harm to the families of the Democrats.
   This is part of the range,
   Including climate change
Of the high wire Biden must walk without safety nets.

Day B-11   1/30/21

The wheels of divisiveness continue to spin
When supremacists threaten their oppositions' kin.
   How many mistakes
   Does it take
For the GOP to learn that healing begins from within?

Day B-12   1/31/21

Tucson recently memorialized Christina Taylor
    Greene,
A child killed by the NRA gun-selling scheme.
    In personal contrast
    We look aghast
At the threats by Congresswoman Marjorie
    Taylor Greene.

Day B-13   2/1/21

The House Republicans have a leadership choice.
They would like to speak with a unified voice.
    Cheney or Taylor Greene
    In the political scene
On the horns of a dilemma they are tossed.

Day B-14   2/2/21

To get their supremacy message across
The far right failed to give Cheney a toss,
   The politically obscene
   Marjorie Taylor Greene,
Wouldn't acknowledge Trump's election loss.

Day B-15   2/3/21

As President Biden continues presidential clarity,
Eric Trump pontificates with some hilarity,
    Claiming to Hannity
    In his political insanity
That his dad exceeds other presidents in popularity.

Day B-16   2/4/21

Biden tosses Trump's last minute nominations,
Pursuing his own duties as the leader of the nation,
But he realizes
That Trump still prizes
The fantasy that he's past all condemnation.

Day B-17   2/5/21

Biden will no longer share intelligence debriefs
With Trump though he was once Commander-in-Chief.
  Biden has won
  And Trump is done,
While the majority of voters sigh a sigh of relief.

Day B-18   2/6/21

David Brooks urged Biden to have a huge
    stimulus package;
Economist Larry Summers warned about too
    much baggage.
  By any measure
  A lot of pressure
From stage managers barking mixed orders back
    stage.

Day B-19   2/7/21

Competing companies could cause Biden to derail
His plans and tell futuristic details they entail;
　All electric cars
　With hope so far
Of putting government policy on the electric upscale.

Day B-20   2/8/21

Biden is under a great deal of political stress
To solve the problems he must now address.
   But still in the news
   Is Trump's short fuse,
As he faces the crimes of which he won't confess.

Day B-21   2/9/21

Biden now needs to take the time to decide
If he will take credit as he sees the pandemic subside.
  We all knew
  As the economy grew
That Trump could take credit only of the country's divide.

Day B-22   2/10/21

Biden puts Trump's foreign policy in reverse;
He will use diplomacy now, chapter and verse.
    Trump had hoped the luster
    Of his inane bluster
Would win him the accolades of the universe.

Day B-23   2/11/21

That Trump incited the insurrectionists' raid
Was the impeachment charge that was made.
   Everyone was tense
   About the defense,
But the GOP seems completely unswayed.

Day B-24   2/12/21

Biden bides his time and stays quite quiet,
Probably just attending to his daily diet
   While Trump screams
   At his legal teams
To disassociate him from the traitors' riot.

Day B-25   2/13/21

GOP senators vote for Trump's acquittal.
President Biden seemed to be noncommittal.
   Of the impeachment trial
   After a short while,
The rest of the world has expressed very little

Day B-26   2/14/21

After the acquittal in the impeachment storm
Biden empathetically calls for gun reform
   Remembering Parkland
   He takes a stand
Against the NRA and their gun sales platform.

Day B-27   2/15/21

Biden must review the policy on immigration,
Considering humanitarian as well as limitation.
   Then the task
   Is to ask
"Does it bring harm or benefit to the nation?"

Day B-28   2/26/21

Biden must now focus on new national unity,
Building a strong and empathetic community.
A person would think
The GOP wouldn't shrink
From their duty to contribute to this renewal opportunity.

Day B-29   2/17/21

In the impeachment, politics are ahead of evidence.
McConnell's vote makes no rational sense,
   Saying Trump was the cause
   But with hardly a pause,
He votes for Trump, while straddling the political fence.

Day B-30   2/18/21

Biden exceeded Trump with his executive orders.
He also opened up many more national borders.
Immigrants already here
Hope citizenship is near,
Anticipating official federal recorders.

Day B-31   2/19/21

Biden today announces, "America is back."
With vaccinations we must get "back on track".
　If that's not enough
　Biden has other stuff.
He must deal realistically with Russian hack.

Day B-32   2/20/21

Biden is certainly not the Donald's biggest fan
He prepares for new nuclear talks with Iran.
   He wants a new deal
     One that is real
Not like the one in effect in Pakistan.

Day B-33   2/21/21

Biden wants more than just getting by;
He's working subreptitiously on the sly.
    He's in a race
    To erase
Any lasting imprints of "that other guy".

Day B-34   2/22/21

Ted Cruz runs when he hears a bit of thunder,
But he blames the media on his latest blunder,
   In running form
   To escape the storm
While continuing to split the GOP asunder.

Day B-35   2/23/21

Biden went to Texas to show presidential empathy
The White House before had expressed little sympathy
   To the nation at large
   Instead had a bully sarge,
Who suffered from a severe case of neuropathy.

Day B-36   2/24/21

Trump's Postmaster General was Louis DeJoy
Who followed Trump's instructions like an office boy.
   Then like a snail
   He slowed down the mail:
Biden will give him a chance for new employ.

Day B-37   2/25/21

Biden named as Energy Secretary, Jennifer Granholm.
In matters of energy she feels quite at home.
   As Michigan's ex-governor
   A position she might've asked for
Another serving opportunity under a capitol dome.

Day B-38   2/26/21

Trump's insurrectionists plot a State of the Union attack.
We thought we'd left the ex-president 38 days back.
His loyal militias
Are certainly malicious,
And Trump is more like an orange jumping Jack.

Day B-39   2/27/21

To make health coverage affordable again
Biden plans changes since the Trumpian reign.
   Biden's heartfelt empathy
   And sincere sympathy
Are on a different presidential plane.

Day B-40   2/28/21

At CPAC Meeting Trump wins the straw poll.
It's not that his popularity is on a new roll.
　When he's not at the helm,
　He doesn't overwhelm.
When he's not winning, he's out of control.

Day B-41   3/1/21

Biden decides not to punish the Saudi Crown
    Prince,
Though the pressure to do so is rather intense
    For the brutal murder
    Of a New York reporter.
Biden's decision doesn't make international good
    sense.

Day B-42   3/2/21

Biden and the Mexican president make pledges of unity,
To avoid treatment of each other's citizens with impunity.
   Like a neighborhood,
   They also could
Have nations form their own extended community.

Day B-43   3/3/21

Some states are abandoning the mandates for masks.
One might wonder about additional medical tasks
   Who loses who wins,
   As the virus needle spins,
While an ominous shadow, across those states, is cast.

Day B-44   3/4/21

March fourth is the date Trump is supposed to
      march forth;
The prediction from Q-Anon for whatever that's
      worth.
   There're folks receiving,
   And apparently believing,
The report that Trumpism will experience an
      international rebirth.

Day B-45   3/5/21

Biden blasts states that abandon mask mandates.
The experts warned the governors of those states.
  Dr. Fauci predicted
  If not interdicted
Those states would experience higher death rates.

Day B-46   3/6/21

President Biden is attempting to go by the book,
Certainly not forgetting the day the world shook,
  While the GOP jokes,
    Calling it a hoax,
The reports that children were killed at Sandy Hook.

Day B-47   3/7/21

For sexual misconduct Governor Cuomo is asked to resign.
He was accused in the work place, to be way our of line.
   He felt the accusation
   Didn't warrant a resignation.
Even top democrats say his actions were less than benign.

Day B-48   3/8/21

Biden has not yet conducted a press conference.
Causing reporters to ask why the unusual suspense,
   Is President Biden
   Perhaps hidin'
Something more than his son's financial offense?

Day B-49   3/9/21

GOP and Dems are considering the filibuster.
Both sides are inclined to pointless bluster.
　　Many are on the fence
　　Which makes no sense
When they need all the clear-headedness, they can muster.

Day B-50   3/10/21

We're half-way through, Biden's first 100 days.
Let's hope that political quiescence actually pays
In the long run.
When we add up the sum,
We'll see how well the political drama plays.

Day B-51   3/11/21

It's almost here; the American Rescue Plan.
Though the GOP are not Biden's greatest fans.
   Now the next task
   To get it to Biden's desk
Before they all sing and dance the burly can-can.

Day B-52   3/12/21

Presidential dogs prompt many citizens to smile.
Biden's dog was punished with a temporary exile.
   He bit someone;
   Not to the bone.
He'll surely return to the White House after awhile.

Day B-53   3/13/21

Trump continues to grab the national headlines.
He bitches and whimpers and rants and whines.
   He never relaxes
   About the election and taxes,
As falsehood and realty he intertwines.

Day B-54   3/14/21

The relief bill should help the working class.
Like stepping through Alice's magic looking glass,
    It's Biden's hope
    That the scope
Of aid will bring them to the Dems' jackass.

Day B-55   3/15/21

Biden is gaining support from small cities and towns.
He's letting them know he won't let them down
   Whether insurance protection
   Or vaccine injection
Plus relief aid to avoid a business shut down.

Day B-56   3/16/21

Biden's legislative addendum may be coming to a
    halt.
To require 60% on legislative bills is actually an
    assault
  On democratic process,
  So Biden must address
The problem, admitting that the filibuster, itself,
    is at fault.

Day B-57   3/17/21

A limerick should fit for the day of St. Patrick;
Whether frustrated diatribe or simply lovesick
   They're often seen
   As truly obscene
They could be nonsense, just like American politics.

Day B-58   3/18/21

GOP voter restrictions revive Jim Crow
    suppression,
They still fear the DEMs' political progression.
    When they restrict the right to vote,
    And diminish the size of the Lifeboat,
Their "Big Tent" diversity was just a political
    expression.

Day B-59   3/19/21

What about Meghan and Harry's unroyal revenge?
Buckingham Palace seems to have become
    unhinged.
  The couple just can't track,
  Going all the way back,
To royal protocol in the age of Stonehenge.

Day B-60   3/20/21

The national economic picture continues to grow,
When in the future will it start to go slow?
   We stand at the financial gates;
   But the Feds won't raise the rates.
We'll take our cues from the Dow Jones show.

Day B-61   3/21/21

This year of the pandemic has been a real bummer.
We're promised vaccination liberation by summer.
   We certainly hope
   That the virus scope
Is not such that it'll be a disappointing late comer.

Day B-62   3/22/21

Even the president's dog may have to be recalled,
But Major must learn the White House protocol.
  If he learns to be calm
  And no more biting harm.
Everything will surely be OK after all.

Day B-63   3/23/21

To have so many killings is certainly no trifle
For demented gun owners with assault rifles.
   We'll let the NRA
   Have their day.
With their Second Amendment rights we must not stifle.

Day B-64   3/24/21

A female soccer player with colorful pink hair,
Told Biden that for girls it just wasn't fair,
   That for women who play
   Should get equal pay,
But women never seem to get their fair share.

Day B-65   3/25/21

What is happening down in Jawgya land?
Legislator are taking their final grand stand.
   They must address
   How to suppress
Citizens from voting in their endangered southland.

Day B-66   3/26/21

Those Georgia crackers showed their legislative
 power
When they passed a hundred-page bill in 24 hours.
 You may already know
 That they're usually slow,
But they can speedily limit the power of their
 ivory Tower.

Day B-67   3/27/21

There's a crucial crisis at our southern borders.
But a silence at the immigration headquarters.
   Too many escaping strife,
   Trying to find a new life.
Kamala Harris must hurry with explicit orders.

Day B-68   3/28/21

Congressman Castro has devised an intelligent plan
To assist southern countries as much as we can
   To improve their agronomy,
   Thus helping their economy,
Reducing drastically the immigration demands.

Day B-69   3/29/21

Biden seems currently to be running ahead.
Many are voting for Bernie Sanders instead.
   A bit of fright
   This Super Tuesday night.
Still counting while everyone is still abed.

Day B-70   3/30/21

We're still saddled with Biden and Son.
What have they nefariously done?
  What waivers
  Or political favors
With Croatia have they established and run?

Day B-71   3/31/21

The Democrats' mammoth Covid stimulus bill
Received a welcome extra boost on the Hill.
   If it's a hit
   Who'll benefit?
The results are still in the political gristmill.

Day B-72   4/1/21

There's a Senate battle over who can vote.
The anxious Democrats are beginning to devote
   Some political expansion
   To West Virginia's Joe Manchin
They're hoping he'll board their expansive boat.

Day B-73   4/2/21

For a sexual crime, Rep. Gaetz, is under investigation,
Involving a 17-year-old girl is the official accusation.
Yet with an ethics so weak,
He's been asked speak
At Women First in America at their annual celebration.

Day B-74   4/3/21

Biden has budgeted some federal programs in the millions $1,000,000.
Other more vital issues have been put in the billions $1,000,000,000.
 The zeroes are scary.
 Certainly inflationary,
The infrastructure budget soars into the trillions, $1,000,000,000,000.

Day B-75   4/4/21

Senate gives powerful tool to work around GOP filibuster
We'll miss that senatorial insignificant bluster.
   Some of the drama will be gone.
   When the filibusterer stands there alone,
The speechifying will have lost some of it luster!

Day B-76   4/5/21

Biden says there's no crisis at the borer.
It should be a concern of the highest order.
  Kids thrown over the wall,
    Some quite small.
Is an international social disorder.

Day B-77   4/6/21

Biden wants to pay $9,000 funeral expense,
For the pandemic victims, which is pure nonsense.
  Dems will be the sacrificial goat;
  The GOP will prattle and gloat
Pointing to the Dems' "tax and spend" sad evidence.

Day B-78   4/7/21

McConnell warns CEOs, to stay out of politics.
You'll just get lost in the Washington mix.
    Stick with something you know
    Not the Bitter Business Bureau
Until we need the next campaign funding "fix".

Day B-79   4/8/21

Iran and US resume nuclear talks.
It won't exactly be a game of tic-toc.
  They shouldn't have stopped
  But Trump had chosen to opt
Out of talks and instead take a political walk.

Day B-80   4/9/21

Google beats Oracle in ten-year suit
But at day's end who really gives a hoot?
   It's about copyright,
   And those who write
Should be dancing more than Rooty toot toot.

Day B-81   4/10/21

Trump attacks McConnell and Pence in "Unity"
   speech.
He attempts to control as far as he can reach.
   McConnell is weak.
   And Pence mustn't speak.
Trump's self-praise religion is what he doth
   preach.

Day B-82   4/11/21

Will we soon have to have proof of immunity?
How will that help build a sense of community?
 TSA checks the planes.
 What if people complain?
How will we achieve a reality of national unity?

Day B-83   4/12/21

In this contentious time, what is life really all about?
Should we sit and sob or instead sing and shout?
   There's a wide scope
   With room for hope.
We've been here before, but never completely struck out.

Day B-84   4/13/21

Biden appointed a new Asian American liaison.
It wasn't that earlier liaisons couldn't be
  depended upon.
It was just the fact
That there was a lack
Of Asian Americans on official upper echelons.

Day B-85   4/14/21

We have regressed back to earlier hateful times
As Congress debates hate-motivated crimes.
   Particularly against Asians
   But also on the occasions
Of others, as reported by the NY Times.

Day B-86   4/15/21

The GOP seems to have another substantial wildfire.
Neither Trump nor Pence is anxious to retire.
　　Trump slams Pence.
　　Pence then hints
That after Biden, he'll be ready for presidential hire.

Day B-87   4/16/21

Biden is tightening US and Europe relations.
Trump had pulled away from other nations,
    Saying, "We don't need any of these."
    Where he wouldn't be "big cheese".
With Russia Biden must make push/pull calibrations.

Day B-88   4/17/21

In foreign policy, Biden makes a practical attempt.
Though holding for his predecessor some
    contempt.
With Putin some sanctions,
    Making Trump more anxious,
He would not in Russian collusion be exempt.

Day B-89   4/18/21

Biden this year will limit migrants to 125,000 admissions.
After that annually only 95,000 will be granted permission
To enter legally,
But less regally,
Others will be coming without legal or practical provisions.

Day B-90   4/19/21

There is concern that there be time limits in the Supreme Court,
And while in office they must refrain from any political effort.
   All federal legislators should also
   Have term limits and not as though
They have lifetime tenure for taxes for support.

Day B-91   4/20/21

The report that financier Bernard Madoff is dead;
Mourned by none, especially those whom he had
   led
   Into a Ponzi scheme,
   Ending his money machine,
No dividends but losses in millions for them
   instead.

Day B-92   4/21/21

Reports of mass shooting have become routine,
Replaced by reports of the coronavirus vaccine.
 The Chauvin conviction
 May show the contradiction
Of "Murder by Police Officer" as recently seen.

Day B-93   4/22/21

We watch a bird on the top of a actus stalk.
He seems to be saying to us. "It's time to talk."
　　"About what?" we ask.
　　"Why of course the task
To come together," as he jumps down and walks the walk.

Day B-94   4/23/21

Ted Cruz says you didn't see Republicans rig the game.
To rig minority voting rights is actually the GOP aim.
   Or "pack the court",
   Which they did of course.
Cruz and Trump should hold hands in the Liars Hall of Fame.

Day B-95   4/24/21

President Biden made a climate comeback now,
To join other world leaders to seek somehow
   "As the world turns"
   To avoid more burns
Unless our national differences we can disavow.

Day B-96   4/25/21

Biden's presidency has less talk more action,
Than the previous administration's stupefaction.
  He continues to strive
  To keep hope alive
Avoiding further political factions.

Day B-97   4/26/21

Arizona GOP continue with falsehoods of the
    election.
As they still rankle form results of voter rejection.
    But Biden plans
    As quick as he can
Assure everyone of protection from future
    insurrection.

Day B-98   4/27/21

Biden's nearing the end of his 100-day sprint.
His policies have elicited little political dissent.
 Who knows tomorrow
 With joy or sorrow
Whether he'll continue to be an ideal president?

Day B-99   4/28/21

Joe Biden in his quiet way seemed to be a tranquilizer.
His address to Congress showed him to be an equalizer
  Of opportunity
  And unity
In everyone sharing as a national community enterprizer.

Day B-100   4/29/21

Biden declares, "America is on the rise anew"
Though with challenges ahead, quite a few.
With health we'll connect
Also without neglect
Infrastructure, immigration, education, 'tis true.

After high school, E. Reid Gilbert pursued education from college to college, culminating in a PhD in Asian Theatre. He has won two Fulbright Awards. His careers have ranged from Methodist Minister to Mime, to Theatre (actor, director, producer and playwright) and University Professor. He is Professor-emeritus of Ohio State University. At age 80 he started a new career as an author and has published ten books plus 10 plays. In addition to this book, he has three more manuscripts nearing completion: EMBODYING THE WORD; GESTURE WITH TEXT Movement Training for Actors: BEYOND THE POWER LINES AND PAVED ROADS, Memoirs of growing up in the NC tobacco hills; THE INNER LIGHT, a poetry collection.

www.ingramcontent.com/pod-product-compliance
Lightning Source LLC
Chambersburg PA
CBHW070930080526
44589CB00013B/1453